Fate, Faith & a Feral Feline

Choose Love

BROOKE BERNARD

AuthorHouse™
1663 Liberty Drive
Bloomington, IN 47403
www.authorhouse.com
Phone: 833-262-8899

Because of the dynamic nature of the Internet, any web addresses or links contained in this book may have changed since publication and may no longer be valid. The views expressed in this work are solely those of the author and do not necessarily reflect the views of the publisher, and the publisher hereby disclaims any responsibility for them.

Any people depicted in stock imagery provided by Getty Images are models, and such images are being used for illustrative purposes only.
Certain stock imagery © Getty Images.

This book is printed on acid-free paper.

ISBN: 978-1-6655-2816-0 (sc)
ISBN: 978-1-6655-2817-7 (hc)
ISBN: 978-1-6655-2815-3 (e)

Library of Congress Control Number: 2021911446

Print information available on the last page.

Published by AuthorHouse 06/04/2021

authorHOUSE

Fate, Faith & a Feral Feline

To: My Mom, Dad, Donald and Collin

They say love reveals itself when you least expect it.
We let love win,
and I am so glad we did.

To anyone who met or knew of Hallie,
Thank You for pouring your love into her.

Contents

Preface

She took the puzzle pieces of her life to form a beautiful masterpiece. Each piece was courageously picked up, seamlessly fit, reflected on, and set down. The puzzle sat out for some time. The pieces uniquely reflected beauty, success, memories, courage, experiences, joy, connection and laughter. Even the pieces of sorrow or challenge played a role in the beauty. The puzzle was incredible and admirable but missing one last piece. *This piece was imminent and sacred to completion before moving forward and starting a new puzzle.* The missing piece was quietly whispering but waited its turn to be liberated. After searching high and low, the piece was found within. This piece was the heart of the puzzle. This book is my puzzle piece, written from the heart. I am overjoyed that you are reading this true story. With love, thank you!

1

Just Start

Dear Hallie,

I walked into the store and saw a notebook with a cover that resembled your lavender color. On the cover of the notebook was written, "Start NOW." It was undoubtedly time to begin this healing adventure. This healing has been a process and brought me to a destination of acceptance, strength, and peace.
I did not have the opportunity to say final goodbyes to you.
I don't have your ashes to spread later in a beautiful flower pot to grow in the sun.
But I do have memories, lessons, and a whole lot of love.
With those gifts, I can water the flowers around me.

I had a dream the night before choosing to publish this book.
You had a dainty chain around your neck. I knew that I needed to unclamp the chain to set you free. You were freed from the chain and lifted into a sorbet, pastel colored sky.
We both needed to be set free.
Here I am, writing and publishing this book.
This book is devoted to you.

My life message is devoted to you.
I embraced you with an open heart and mind.
There are no guarantees in life.
If the love is there,
if even for a brief moment,
embrace the love with all of your being.
Do your best in all situations.

This story touches on all the four types of love recognized by the ancient Greeks.
Eros, (romantic love.)
Philia, (friendship as love.)
Storge, (familial love.)
Agape, (universal love.)

My wish is that your spirit will enlighten the person who has picked
up this book. The message and themes will take the reader on a path
of elements with joy, loss, grief, resilience and triumph.
After all, the universe works in mysterious ways to thread life events and relationships.
There are many concepts that may take some reflection and endurance to
connect through symbolism, stories, questions to ponder and faith.
The messages may be unique to each induvial that has picked up this book.
The thoughts that arise deserve to be felt and elevated.

My wish is that the reader always chooses love.
Love, Brooke

2
Hour Glass on the Heart

Would you choose love if you knew it was going to be short-lived?
Would you choose love if it knocked then walked through the door,
heart-swelling,
twirled you around,
and swept you off your feet,
only to fade away.
In the words of John Mayer, would you choose love while
"slow dancing in a burning room?"
Would you choose love if you knew it had the potential for strengthening
bonds between loved ones, maintaining connections and bringing
joy and laughter, though it could end in sheer heart break?
Would you choose love through a yearning last breath?
As the sand of love timely pours through the heart of an hourglass,
would you still choose love?
Do you believe that in the end, love triumphs all?

What if I told you that your life would change overnight by taking
a chance at love? If you had no idea what was to arise, would
you put your heart on the line and take the chance?
Are you relentless in your pursuit to capture love in all
areas of your life, even towards yourself?
With light, there is dark; and with dark, there is light.
After all, the darkest part of night is before the sun rises.
There will be moments of pausing to catch your breath in
overwhelming beauty, revival, contemplation, or sorrow.
I am here to tell you: through these inevitable life patterns and forces,
choose love, always.

3

Vacancy

My apartment was silent on a dark Sunday night in January of 2016.
The background noise of carpet sprints and floor pitter-patters was
absent. Emptiness and fear set in. *"Hallie is gone!,"* I thought.
Little did I know that this exact empty and vacant feeling would become
permanent on July 8, 2019.
It would take love to fill that vacancy to fulfillment.

Hallie, the feral feline, had quite the way of bringing life back to perspective through
her attention-seeking antics. That dark and drawn-out January evening, she hid
her petite, kitten body in the crevice of the counter from below. After I called out
to Hallie in panic for many hours, searching every nook and cranny and convinced
she was stolen, she let out a delicate sneeze that could be heard only by an angel.
I turned on my phone flashlight and began scanning the nooks.
Suddenly, her eyes caught the reflection of the light.
Her big eyes peered out from deep under the counter as if to say *"Gotcha!"*
After I ripped out the plywood with feverish haste thinking she was
stuck, in typical Hallie fashion she pranced her way out for some loves.

She was in the crevice of the counter all along. If I had reflected in calm and listened to my gut, I potentially might have found her sooner. Through her interruptions, Hallie had a way of teaching us the importance of the life "pause" and using our senses.

Her antics were real,
her spirit was bold and boundless,
and my home and heart will never be the same.

Dear Hallie,

After this evening, it was suggested that I take you back to the local animal shelter. You were trouble and feral. I knew the tide was rolling in after this evening. I had met my match. However, I still chose to take a chance at love. My life was about to be forever changed. You were here to stay and I held space for you every step of the way.

4

To Gather and Connect

The concept of the *rainbow bridge* is an iridescent place that pets cross upon death
from the physical world, to eventually be reunited with their owners. As the pet
departs the physical world into heaven, they begin a beautiful journey of restoration.
The concept of the rainbow bridge helps people adjust to mourning or bereavement.
When Hallie called out for me three and a half years ago, I had no way of knowing
that she would be the physical and authentic version of a rainbow bridge. Even before
her departure, she was the true connector between loved ones in this physical world.
The name Hallie is short for the word *"Hallelujah."*
Additionally, the name Hallie refers to a gathering place or "hall."
The well-known song, "Hallelujah" composed by Leonard Cohen is about *love and
loss*. When I chose Hallie's name, I simply just believed it to be a beautiful name. Only
after her passing, did I make the connection with the verified meaning of her name.
This was not planned.
Hallie had an exceptional spirit and a way of gathering and
connecting family and friends. She crossed each *"bridge"* throughout
town in her carrier from one location to the next.
I had unwavering trust that she would be cared for, loved and protected at her destinations.

I had unwavering trust, that my heart too would be held, as she was an extension of me.
She enjoyed cathartic car rides with her stuffed animal "ducky" only to be embraced
with enthusiasm, passion and open arms at her next location by loved ones.
Hallie, or "Halz," had many "palz." She greeted with squeaks, hugs, taps,
darts, and butterfly kisses. She melted for the people and places she loved.
Hallie was the *"baby of the family."*
We poured our hearts into her and she returned that love like a melody
five times over.
My two brothers would gently rock Hallie like a baby, singing the song
"Three Little Birds" by Bob Marley.
I would watch them and giggle, but really my heart was bursting with love and gratitude.
One brother would sing in a low, soothing, but sarcastic voice.
The other would chime in with his own commentary and ways with Hallie.
Hallie eased into their voices, having fun and swaying in rhythm.
These lyrics were in many ways a premonition of what was to come.
At the time, who would have known? The angels, probably.

Rise up this mornin'

Smiled with the risin' sun (Sun)

The three little birds (Birds)

Pitch by my doorstep…. (Steppy!)

Singin' sweet songs (Sweeeet songs)

Of melodies pure and true (True)

Sayin"...
This is my message to you.

With loss, you learn how to appreciate antics, nuisances, and messes.
Anyone with a pet understands the torn-up rugs and toilet paper, the
hair, the responsibility, - but all the messes are a sign of life.
Where there is a sign of life, there is love prescnt.
Now we have clean spaces, but for what purpose?
How could such a petite, feral animal have such a profound spirit and live daily truth?
Well, Hallie was created for us. She had collections of ground
to gather, cover and connect with a strong purpose.
Fate and faith interwove and united us.
Hallie-lujah!
Are you willing to pitch by the doorstep and choose love?

5

The Wait

Hallie's story began in December of 2015. We had just put to rest our family cat of eighteen years, Callie. I was not ready to love another animal. Callie had my heart. One day after Christmas, I had "kitten fever" and started browsing the local animal shelter website.
"Cumulus," Hallie's original name, struck me with her sunshine, golden eyes. She was three months old and was the size of my palm. My dad and I shared a mutual love for cats, but he quickly shut the idea of another animal down.
Adhering, I dismissed the idea as well.
One month later, January of 2016 approached.
On that Saturday morning,
"Cumulus" crossed my mind again.
I was on the elliptical at the gym working out with some friends. With all the "noise" around me, in some way I felt Hallie call out to me. That moment, I reached for my phone with the battery at 10% and immediately called the animal shelter to see if she was still available. I was told she was in another town, only to be called back indicating she was down the street in Reno.
I thought to myself,

"This kitten is perfect. How has she not been adopted?"
Within twenty minutes, I was en route to track her down.
Jesus literally took the wheel. Although there were many obstacles in
the process of meeting her, I was persistent during each visit.
She was patiently waiting for me.
When you are being called, are you willing to choose and act on love?

6

Intuition

Written in the stars, destiny, supernatural power, we have
all heard of these sayings in one form or another.
I like to call this, "fate."
Fate stops you in your tracks.
There is not always an explanation, but always a greater feeling of
"inner knowing."
My tracks came to a halt with tears of overwhelming
love, joy, and intuition when I met Hallie.
She was held tightly, wrapped in a red towel like a "purr-itto."
She gazed up at me and with exhilaration, our hearts chorded.

My soul recognized Hallie and I followed my intuition like a compass.
My breath was swiftly taken away. I was aligned with love and purpose. I acted
cautiously at first, aware of her being so feral, but deep down I was all in.
The animal shelter was very protective and secretive about Hallie.
She had this deep gaze in her eyes of mischief and fear.
However, behind this gaze of fear, she was deeply longing for love.

I recognized that deep look in her eyes. Unknowingly at the time, Hallie was a reflection of that feeling I had within myself. In the process of wanting to rescue and save her from that feeling, there was a duality that I was freeing my own longing within.

Aren't we all on a quest for love?

By listening to intuition, does fate leads us to love?

The shelter gave me every reason not to pursue her. Truly, I believe they were testing my tenacity because they wanted the right fit for her. My personality is relentless when I truly believe in a purpose and I could not fathom life without her.

When being tested, do you give up or keep pursuing?

After multiple visits, bringing very special people with me along each time, we eventually became the Brookie and Halz pair of Reno.

She was meant for me.

I was meant for her.

We were in each other's blueprints and a vibrational match.

She was meant for everyone.

She was revealing to me what needed to be renewed within.

Are you willing to listen to your intuition, follow it like a compass and choose love?

7

Muddy Boots

Cumulus; latin word for "layer."
Cumulus was Hallie's original name.
Hallie broke through all layers of the human emotions.
As stated by my grandmother, *"Her fur has beautiful markings."*
After all, we called her *"Muddy Boots."*
The muddy boots resembled her dark ashy feet, as if she
had trotted through a chimney of charcoal.
I often wondered the prestigious dust she trotted through in a previous life.
It is no coincidence that Hallie broke down our emotional layers with those
muddy boots of hers, leaving her trailed "mark "on countless hearts and lives.

When you love a person or animal, conversation and commotion is often
derived around that distinct soul. When that connection disappears, the space
is absorbed with silence and inquiry. The name of the soul and their movement
within the empty space carries an element of echo, gravity, and attention.
"Hallie." With deeper assertion, *"Hallie."*
What is the name that reverberates for you?

We all have that specific name in our lives. Just the sound of a name can send your heart off fluttering with confidence or take you back on the ride of a sinking ship in the ocean of emotion. With the reverberating sound, depth is felt with a trailed mark on your heart and surroundings.

What role of love did this soul play in your life?

Eros, (romantic love.)
Philia, (friendship as love.)
Storge, (familial love.)
Agape, (universal love.)

This soul is a part of your daily routines and thought patterns.
We are all made up of the places we frequent and people we meet and commiserate with along the way. We mutually leave a little bit of ourselves and pick up something new, oftentimes with a whisper of magic.
These presences are engrained in the intricacies of our lives.

The trailed mark can be as smooth as how you drink your coffee in the morning...
To how you drive back roads home with the sun setting...
Or as intimate as how you say your prayers before going to sleep at night.

Where are the intricate, trailed marks in your life?

Sometimes, you want to leave the muddy marks because the marks are all you have left.
You would rather keep the marks, than have nothing at all.
The marks become a referencing point,
hold a place in time,
and become a piece of your identity.
Are you willing to get a little muddy and choose love?

8

Commonalities

It is common that pets often resemble their owners, but
how often are their personalities the same, too?
Hallie and I were parallel in many traits.
Blonde, sparkling eyes, radiant and petite.
Hallie, like myself, leaned on the side of feral;
suggestive, unpredictable, fierce, with a hint of wild.
In the attempts to domesticate Hallie, her spirit was every bit of feral.
Though there was much resemblance, Hallie intimidated me at first. She was untamed
in this little body. She was busy, unique, adventurous, and truly had a mind of her own.
Nonetheless, the first morning after bringing her home, she
tapped me with her left paw on my hand with assurance.
Ironically, I am a leftie too.
I knew instantly that with her leftie love tap, she was mine, and I was hers.
She tapped me into her life.

In my dad's words, "*Hallie was a lover, a people's person, and wanted to be a
part of the action. She was very trustworthy and loyal once she knew you.*"

Amongst many commonalities, trust and loyalty were the
most prominent traits that Hallie and I shared.
We both cautiously invested our time to the souls our hearts were drawn to.
We knew where love was needed.
This level of trust introduced her to many amazing people in my life.
Through these introductions and interactions, trust,
loyalty, and love were always at the core.
When the love isn't initially tame,
are you still willing to choose love?

9

The First Stop

The simplicity of a laundry room floor in January of 2016.
Your childhood home.
Your dad.
A timid feral kitten that was supposedly sick.
A strong advising not to hold her for a couple of days.
A shared love for felines.
The room filled with an energy of love, admiration, and overwhelming
connection as we lay on our stomachs on the ground.
We were in awe of her alluring presence.

Those "*muddy boots*" of hers were making that mark on us.

A petite, feral feline brought this profound love.
Hallie would later leave this world shortly after, twelve days before my dad's accident.
However, she would not fail to remind us of her presence that evening of the accident.
In Hallie's unique manner, she found a way that evening
to demonstrate the love she had for all of us.
Would you choose love and freely share it?

10
Lavender Ridge

The color lavender represents creativity, optimism, free spirited and youthfulness.
After Hallie's "first stop" in 2016, we drove to my
apartment past a place called Lavender Ridge.
Lavender Ridge's colors consist of yellow/gold and lavender. While
driving by, I revealed all the wonderful people Hallie was going to meet
in this life. Upon her passing, this location and color would represent
a piece of faith and strength three and a half years later.

We all have been at "ridges" in our lives.
Hopefully, you have had support along your way.
Hallie was by my side as I trekked ridges and the elevation kept getting higher.
However, when trekking the ridges, you are that much closer to heaven.
Heaven was above me.
Heaven was beside me.

The night of Hallie's passing, I had a vivid dream.
In the dream, there were two beautiful and pure feathers,
each flawlessly in their own separate bags.

One feather was lavender and the other was gold.

I had always wondered what Hallie's "color" would be.

One week prior to her sudden passing, my mom and I discussed the representation of colors and auras. Callie, our old cat's color was "golden."

This evening in my dream, I was confident that Hallie spoke to me.

She shared with me that her color was lavender, and she was now with Callie.

When at a ridge, will you look above, beside or within and choose love?

Dear Hallie,

Do you remember your first official ride in the car passing Lavender Ridge when I brought you home? The moment felt like bringing a baby home from the hospital. You had the world in front of you as you peered out the window, leaning into your blanket with comfort and awe. So many people were ready to love you. You had just met mom and dad. Then, I explained that you were soon going to meet your brothers, cousins, grandparents, aunts, uncles, and friends. I proclaimed that you were petite, strong, and beautiful. My heart swelled with the love and enthusiasm I had for you.

11

Outstretched for Love

We all have a love language that resonates with our needs.
This language may consist of words of affirmation, act of service,
receiving/giving gifts, quality time and physical touch.
What is your love language?
It is important to recognize that we do not all have the same love
language. Sometimes the best act of love is taking the others into
consideration through action.
Noticing the details or remembering the little things that are important.
Humans and animals alike crave love through their language,
especially Hallie.
Hallie showed up for me.
I showed up for her.

Feeling seen and acknowledged with our language
carries us through the light and darkness of life.
During Hallie's first of couple days, she outstretched for love with her
paws and feet, just wanting to be acknowledged and loved on.

However, being that she was sick, I was not able to hold or pet her.

For days, Halz squeaked, tapped, and sniffled.

Anything to catch my attention. She had to be the center of it.

Our connection and bond were conjoined at the core of our souls and grew during this time when physical touch was not an option. When I was finally able to hold her, I knew the love language unique to her personality,

the physical out stretch.

In the flow of life, I

o u t s t r e t c h e d

to her too.

Are you willing to choose love when there are barriers?

12

You Are My Sunshine

"Rise up this mornin'
Smiled with the risin' sun."

Three and a half years. Three and a half years, every morning Hallie
started my day at four o'clock before the sun began to arise.
Darting, pouncing, sprinting.
She had me smilin'.
This time was sacred to us.
Time and presence are sacred in all relationships.
With deliberate intention, time and small actions matter most;
An extra thirty minutes to sip coffee before the hustle of the day,
An extra mile on a walk together,
A hand-written note on a napkin, tucked away to find later,
Saving the last bite of dessert,
One last dance.
It is showing up.

To this day, I can still hear Hallie's carpet darts and feel her pounces
over my body, only to end with a soft tap of her paw to
"wake up."
She was also expressing,
"Tag, you're it."
"Show up."
"Are you going to choose love today?"
Somehow, she intuitively caught the alarm every morning
right before ringing. She held me accountable.
Three and a half years, facing some grey days. Some very joyful days. Some very over-
extended days while trying to establish my independence and direction. However, I
knew Hallie's petite, but strong demeanor would greet these days specifically with a
ray of sunshine for me. She poured light into me. Just as the golden sun rises every day,
Hallie was a guaranteed constant in my life, amidst consistent changes and seasons.
Hallie represented everything beautiful, golden, and free in the world, just like
a rainbow bridge and sunshine. There is no coincidence that she entered my life
at the beginning of significant chapters and left as I was about to embark a new
one. She strongly served her purpose that carries me all the days of my life.
Are you willing to "rise up" and choose love?

Dear Hallie,

You are my still sunshine. You represented warmth, light, and redemption.
Your eyes were golden that reflected the sun in your soul. Not only
will you always be my sunshine, you are everyone's sunshine.
You made us happy when skies were grey.
You knew dear, how much we loved you.
Your eternal sunshine will never be taken away.

13

Papillion

Tuesday, August 27, 2019- *"Ever since Hallie met the big man upstairs, I've seen nothing but yellow pretty butterflies. Butterflies will always be the way I remember her now. Butterfly in French is called Papillion and that's the title of one of my favorite movies."*
Hallie loved everyone, but especially melted for my youngest brother. He has a calm nature that allowed Hallie to lean into tranquility. He would pick her up and cradle her in a cocoon. In a deep voice, his brief but powerful words murmured, *"OHHH, Halzzzzz."*
Hallie thought she hit the jackpot with the attention she received from him. Hallie was distinguishable to an alluring *"yellow pretty butterfly."* When you needed her, she had a way of spreading her wings and playing games. In her feral nature, she was elegantly uncatchable, just like a yellow or golden butterfly.
Like a butterfly, Hallie was drawn to light and chased all glimpses.
She would later grow her true wings.
Are you willing to follow the light and choose love?

14

What Do You See?

When you look in the mirror, what do you see?
How do you perceive yourself?
What is in your field of vision?
Are you willing to stop and gaze, uses your senses, and transcend
the magnitude of your presence that others notice?
Hallie often peered at her reflection in a magnified mirror,
viewing herself as big, courageous and a lion.
Though she was petite, she had a prevailing soul and presence.
When she spent time with my dad, he spoke to her in the mirror about life. Some days
as humans, we do not want to face ourselves and even Hallie certainly had her finicky
moments. Regardless, on the days he spoke to her, she let out her *"political purr"* and
leaned into his words. As their reflections were mirrored back, he shared words of
kindness, working hard, life enthusiasm, and making smart choices. The evenings that
Hallie spent with my mom, she embraced lessons on self-care and was nurtured.
Hallie truly did not have one bad day. In fact, her days and purpose were so fulfilled
she never used one of her *"cat"* lives. The one life that she had, she covered her ground.
She was a force to be reckoned with and had the spirit that all humans should embody.

As my alarm memo flashes every morning still at four o'clock, "*Live Like Halz*" is my daily mantra and devotion. She taught me how to show up for myself, look in the mirror and step into my power. I set the intention to conquer the world in her honor with courage, every day.

Are you willing to look in the mirror, make a smart choice, and choose love?

Dear Hallie,

You never saw yourself as small. You never cowered down to anything.
You were larger than life.
You lived in the present moment.
You glanced at yourself in the mirror with intent and truth.
I take your spirit with me every day.
If I don't "Live Like Halz"… my daily purpose has not been fulfilled.

15

Pounce

"C'mon, c'mon, c'mon....oooohhh"
I would say with encouragement.
3-2-1
Halz pounces.
Halz was a calculated risk taker. When she pounced, she was
a force. Sunshine, golden eyes dilated and focused.
Low to the ground. Heart fiercely and passionately pounding.
Swaying her body and leaning into the pounce with determination.
If you going to pursue something in life, recognize the support and
encouragement behind you and be like Halz, passionately pounce!
Pounce with purpose!
Pounce with devotion!
Pounce with focus!
Pounce with conviction!
Pounce with fortitude!
Pounce with love!
Pounce, and do not look back.

In times of rest, rest hard. Find your space. Bask in the sunlight like Halz. Take your time and re-establish yourself for the next pounce.

Are you willing to recognize when it is time to pounce and choose love?

16

Feather

Feathers, fate, faith, family and a feral feline.

"Accept the things to which fate binds you and love the people with whom fate brings you together but do so with all of your heart."
–Marcus Aurellius

Hallie had a knack for playing with goose feathers. She would not choose just any feather though. The feathers were often sturdy and vertical, pointing straight up to the heavens. Additionally, I have always believed that a feather observed is a sign that an angel is near. On the warm Sunday evening of July 7, 2019 the day before Hallie's sudden passing, I took a summer walk and came across a beautiful, taintless black and white goose feather on the trail. The uniqueness of this feather was alerting me. I took a moment to examine it and then released it back to nature.

Days before, I dropped Hallie off at my parents.
I was not aware that these would be the last moments I would spend with her.
That is the thing about life,
we rarely have the foresight of when a last moment will be.
With a family member.
A friend.
A lover.
A pet.

Last goodbyes.
Last laughs.
Last kisses.
Last shared meals.
Last embraces.
Last words.
Last footsteps, trotting away around the corner.
I can see and feel this so vividly.
These lasts can only be returned during times of nostalgia.

Like molasses on the heart to work through,
these lasts are soul aching, and the remorse is often heavy.

We place so much value on memories.
They are so close yet so far.
With reflection, the memory was perfect in that present moment.
Most moments are uniquely made for us.

If you could go back to a pivotal "last" moment,
Would you remember your words and actions?

Would you say what needed to be said?
Would you greet or send off with affirmative action and sincerity?
Would you slow the moment down to savor?
What would you do differently?
But most importantly, would you love a little harder?

Monday morning, July 8, 2019 at seven o'clock,
I called my mom to check on Hallie. I had been having depicting dreams
and I knew intuitively something was not right that summer morning.
I gently asked,
"Does Hallie need to go to the vet?"
"Is she happy?"
My mom assured me that Hallie was perfectly fine and was enjoying a beautiful
summer morning. Before enjoying the morning though, she was peering out
the window with intent and determination. Animals have that sense to feel
energy and hear sounds that humans do not have the ability to experience.
Something was calling Hallie outside of that window.
Just at the right moment, she bolted out the door.
This was extremely uncharacteristic of her.
After bolting, she received a little scolding.
She received the scolding to ensure a bolting incident did not happen again.
The scolding was an act of love and protection.

Was the scolding the last words that Hallie heard?

Ironically, I had a house cleaner come over that morning to my place. I
did not connect at the time that with some messes in the home,
comes a sign of life and love.

One hour later from the phone call, I went to the vet and bought Hallie new food, in hopes to reverse this awful feeling I had. I went out for my summer morning walk, straight from the purchase at the vet. As I was walking, I came across the same exact, pure looking beautiful feather as the day before in a gutter.

I took a moment to observe it and snapped a picture.

I thought to myself,

"Why was this feather in my pathway again?"

Thirty minutes later, to the time of the food purchase
receipt, I received a phone call from my dad.

"Brooke, where are you?"

"Before I say anything more, I need you need to sit down right now."

"I want you to know that we did everything we could."

"Hallie………….."

To this day I cannot finish the sentence and chills go up my spine.

With each word my dad spoke, my stomach dropped.

All I can say, with absolute certainty, is that an *angel promptly swooped her up.*

I walked back to the vet and returned the food.

Never, would I have imagined, the magnitude of this
inconsolable moment during the exchange.

The exchange of any item defines an end.

The empty space brings reality into existence.

The receipt from the return became a symbol of the price I paid to love.

Hours later, I returned to find the feather observed from
my morning walk, still in the gutter unscathed.

This time, I picked up the feather for my own safe keeping and memory.

This feather was pointing straight up to heaven.

This feather I came across in the gutter moments before the call from my dad, I can say again with certainty, was Hallie's sign to me that she had crossed the *rainbow bridge* that very moment I first saw it that morning.

She was now flying with the angels.

She touched the sky.

My knees hit the ground.

The hourglass of love with her presence on earth had reached the passage of time.

I paused and was numb,

filled with contrasting beauty, grief, and awe.

A few hours later, my dad and I went to lunch. He was the only person that I could be in the presence of and speak to. He was my strength as I was shattered. We all were shattered and trying to process what had happened. However, if anyone knew this heart break with the mutual love for cats, it was my dad. We sat outside at a restaurant. As I tried to stomach soup on a hot summer day, we spoke of memories, holding back deep tears of grief.

When we walked back to our cars after lunch, we came across a feather mural.

Again, Hallie profoundly spoke.

I aimlessly drove home to my clean and silent apartment.

I walked through the door;

Just like that, there were no more squeaks.

There was no more pouncing.

There were no more floor pitter-patters.

There was no more purring.

There were no messes,

nor a sign of life or love left from my favorite soul in this world.

All that I had left were tears, a feather, faith, and memories unique to my heart.

In the words of Leo Christopher, *"Home is wherever you leave everything you love and never question that it will be there when you return."*
Unfortunately, at that time, I had reason to question. I had a deep fear of loss and departure. My home felt foreign to me. The walls that had absorbed the life Hallie and I shared held many tales. They were now barren, deeply absorbing the absence of presence.

Whether it be empty walls,
an empty corner of a cabinet,
an empty drawer,
big or small...
How do you consolidate this empty space that was once filled?

As foreign as "home" felt though, I wanted to lean into that feeling and those walls. Hallie was still a part of my identity with her trailed mark on my heart. I began saying "thank you" every time I left home because sometimes, you just never know. It took time to fill those walls with acceptance, having the confidence and courage to create new memories that would fill that space again.

With even more time and experience, I gathered the strength and inner knowing
when it was time to inhabit a new space and move on from those walls.
Being sentimental is a defining trait,
but there is a delicate dance between holding on and letting go.
Sometimes, you need someone to patiently take you by
the hand and dance with you through it.

Home is within.
Love is within.

Just like the quote, I found that both will always be
there when you have the desire to return.

*My heart came to terms that I could still carry my roots with me and water them
wherever I was meant to go in this life.
The roots can grow on the bridge from the past to a new present.*

***Dear Hallie,
You were the rainbow bridge in this life. You were the connector. You have
now crossed the rainbow bridge into heaven, what a beautiful thing. You are
home. Heaven now knows how much I loved you, always and forever.
You have bridged me towards new chapters.
I understand you will always be with me.***

17

Birds of a Feather, we...

The summer of 2019 had its trials. That summer was a defining moment in
time for a multitude of reasons. Twelve days after Hallie grew her wings, my
dad had a sudden accident. Our worlds were suddenly set back again. We had
to band together as a family without our rainbow bridge connecter, Hallie.
The evening that my dad came home from the hospital, it
was the most still night of air of the summer.
It was what we would call, a *"Hallie Evening."*
The only difference about this evening involved the blue
jay that befriended Hallie over the years.
This blue jay that we had not seen in two weeks since Hallie's
passing was squawking loudly as the sun was setting.

The little bird was,
pitched by the doorstep,
singing sweet songs of melodies pure and true.

Hallie was obviously not anywhere physically in sight.
She left this beautiful world twelve days prior.

We all took notice of the blue jay, but mostly of the absence of Hallie.
We went inside, the dismay was too real between the loss
of Hallie and the transpiring's of the accident.

Five minutes later, my mom came outside to find the most
pristine,
beautiful,
petite
and
graceful white feather laying flat, directly in front of the sliding door.
The white feather glistened with the sunset back drop.
There was not a breath of wind in the air.
She went inside to show my brothers and within minutes,
the feather had vanished with distinct brevity.

There was no reason for the blue jay to be squawking so defining.
During this moment, *my family and I flocked together.*

Was the feather a visitation from our petite and pure Angel Hallie?
Was the feather sent for love and comfort?
Was this a reminder to choose love and belief that there is something greater than us?

Dear Hallie,

Thank you. We now know that you are with us, always.
WE LOVE YOU.

18
Grief Is

Grief is an abundance of love and not having a place for it to go. Grief is shock.
Grief is tears. Grief is anger. Grief is disbelief. Grief is sleepless nights.
Grief is getting out of bed in the morning, only to step in the same puddle.
When is the puddle going to dry?
Will it ever fully dry?
Grief is not just over a singular incident.
It is a process of memories fading away, dreams
shattered and adjustments to life's detours.
It is new routines, belief systems altered and how your heart resonates with the world.
Sometimes there are words,
Other times, there is silence.

Have you ever used glitter and unexpectedly found remnants weeks or months later?
Grief shows up like glitter in those weeks and months when you thought it was cleaned
up. You notice that shine and glimmer of the glitter. Sometimes your grief takes you
back and other times you can objectively look at the emotions and let them pass.

Grief is staring out a window with wandering eyes, waiting for Hallie with an energy of anticipation to run up to the door. Grief is walking through the door after a long day, feeling an absence of her at your feet. Grief is avoiding places she would bask in the sun. Grief is putting away the last toy of hers that you found months later under the couch, knowing you will not be opening that cabinet again for a long time. Grief is avoiding adjusting back the doorstop caps that she would fling around. Grief is rolling over in the middle of the night without your best friend by your side or above your head like a guardian angel.
Grief is finding little annoyances and messes as blessings now.

Grief is running a race on Hallie's birthday in 2019; rugged terrain with tears streaming from your eyes that blend in with the rain. Thunder rolling throughout the mountains and telling yourself, *"Hallie Spartan Spirit"* to conquer the physical pain with strength. After all, in my mom's words, *"Hallie had the spirit of a Spartan."*

Grief is sharing the memories of Hallie with people who did not even know her. These people demonstrating love for her through flowers, cards, listening, trinkets and "cheers," simply because she was so special to me.

That is the thing about love, there is always a rainbow bridge that connects.

Grief expands and shrinks with how the sun sits in the sky. Grief is the seasons changing; the sun setting on summer and the fall air settling in. The sunflowers you walked past every day since July 8, 2019 to cope, now a barren brown field. Grief is finding a dainty piece of black and white

(dark and light) fur,
reminding yourself to always lean into the "light."
Grief is now praying to the angels that they are taking good care of
your twin soul, knowing that she has separation anxiety.
Grief is making a wish on a dandelion that your heart
will be filled from vacancy to fullness again.
As you blow away the pedals, you trust the winds will
cleanse the grief and carry your wish.

Through the thick and thin moments,
there is a beautiful duality between
grief and healing.
Grief changes how you view and interact with the world.
When you are healing, you make changes and a transformation occurs.
With healing, the puddle begins to dry, bit by bit.
Some moments are bitter and some are sweet.

The tug of war rope is dropped.
Hands burning and hurting.
You have identified with that pain.
Your hands are now free though.
There is now opportunity for rebirth.

The grief is tucked away with a beautiful, sturdy lock
paired with a unique key.

You get to business living.

Healing brings connection.

With connection, you discover reasoning and purpose.
You move throughout the world different,
oftentimes with more grace and ease.
You acknowledge that life unfolds for the highest good of all.
Love, loss and healing are catalysts for internal and external growth.
Hallie was a healer and the "*CATalyst*" in my life and journey.
Through the thick and thin moments of grief, are you still willing to choose love?

19

Tunes of an Angel

Love is protecting the ones you adore. Love is wanting to provide all experiences and the best things in life. Love is zealously nurturing. Love is security. Love is trust. Love is time. Love is forgiveness. Love is connection. Love is vulnerability.
Love is showing up in the moment and place where it is needed most.
However, love cannot be tamed.
It cannot settle in a cage.
Even with the best intentions of the hand extending nurture and protection,
it cannot be leashed.
Love is not controlled.
Love will always invite you to step into your purpose.
Love may be right outside of your window, waiting for you.

*The one you love may hear a different tune outside of their own window,
just like Hallie heard.*
Therefore, love must be set free and surrendered.

Was Hallie's purpose to teach lessons of choosing love, separating,
and investigating the true meaning of life to bring unification?

There is a belief in the universe that when an angel is near, their
appearance is profound, brief and one just "knows."
The angels often send signs and gifts.
I have received harmonious sounding "angel tokens" being
dropped in my ear while in a deep sleep.
I have received "Phantom" water drops.
And most beautifully, I received Hallie.
Hallie was our physical and true angel on earth for three and a half
short years.
She was a gift.

*And one day, in a blink of an eye, another angel played a tune and came to
claim her.*

No matter how deeply she was loved, protected or cocooned,
she was called.
Hallie's wings grew and she sought the sky.
Hallie was love. Hallie was the lesson. Hallie was the Rainbow Bridge.

Dear Hallie,

Today is July 8, 2020. It has been three hundred and sixty-five days
that you have resided in heaven. This is my final letter to you.
*Time has brought the power of acceptance of the events that unfolded but I
understand that I will always holding your passing gently- and that is okay.*

I envision you sprinting with joy throughout endless green fields, making
your mark in your "muddy boots" on heaven's land. I imagine the warm
rays of the sun soaking up your golden eyes and filling your soul. I envision
you chasing light and playing with goose feathers. I imagine your beautiful
wings sending you on heaven's adventures with your new best friends.
It makes my heart happy to know that I will see you again some day.
As I reflect further on your purpose, my take-away is the importance
of big love in small everyday moments in all relationships.
This means hugging tighter.
Being present.
Saying a person's name with warmth.
Sharing laughter and tears.
Filling in the gaps where love is needed.
Showing up.
Recognizing the fragility of life
…………

Your spirit lives within me in my day-to-day actions,
with love being at the core of it all.
Grief is often the final gift of love between souls.
However, choosing to live out love is going to be my final yet infinite gift to you.

You motivate me, guide me and will always be with me.

The message and challenge that I have learned from you is to choose love, every day.

<u>Fate</u> united us. <u>Faith</u> unites us.

My fur angel, **<u>feral feline</u>,**

we will remain

unitedly.

20

The Challenge

When we looked at Hallie, we saw heaven. We saw truth. We saw joy.
We saw forgiveness. We saw light. And we were restored.
She was a miracle.
Now, the challenge is to hold onto this restoration without
her physical body, but with her eternal spirit.
Throughout Hallie's short life, she told us big things in little ways, daily.
I have been challenged through life's twists and turns after Hallie and often
remind myself to humbly choose love over fear in all situations.
We do not always know the outcome of choosing love.
But in the end,
one cannot go wrong by staying open and choosing love,
whether for yourself or another.

Hallie's end point was just the beginning of a lifelong challenge.

Where does the love pour into now though?
What can be created in this new space?

I have found that her spirit lives on in all spaces with bravery in daily choices, challenges, and commitments.

3-2-1.....
Tag, you are it.
The hourglass has been reset.
It is time to follow your intuition like a compass.
It is time to pounce.
It is time to chase the light.
It is time to rise up.
It is ok to get a little muddy.
There is a tune outside of your window.
Be the things you love most about those who have touched your life.
Share those things freely.

Choose love.
Fate & faith takes over from here.
Expect Miracles.
Hallie-lujah.

"Have enough courage to trust love one more time and always one more time." –Mary Angelou

Will you continue to choose love through this challenge?

About the Author

Brooke Elizabeth Bernard is the author behind "Fate, Faith & a Feral Feline." (ig: @Brooke_Bernard)

She is a Middle School Teacher with deep Nevadan roots.

Brooke earned her Bachelor's & Master's Degree in Education at the University of Nevada, Reno.

Her inspiration came for this book by rising with the sun, coffee in hand and running miles on the trail.

Time spent playing the piano provided the imagery for the written words.

She values faith, wellness & connection…leaning into twists of adventure, laughter & fun.

She is a passionate life-long learner, ambitious and embraces new experiences.

Brooke believes in the magic of life & is confident that choosing love will always bring your heart's desire.

CPSIA information can be obtained
at www.ICGtesting.com
Printed in the USA
LVHW070835291221
707423LV00009B/242